THE LUNGS AND BREATHING

Revised Edition

Steve Parker

Series Consultant
Dr Alan Maryon-Davis
MB, BChir, MSc, MRCP, FFCM

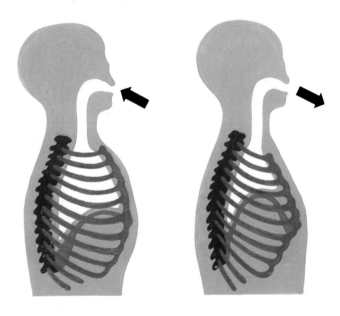

Franklin Watts

London • New York • Toronto • Sydney

© **1989 Franklin Watts**

Original edition first published in 1982
First Paperback Edition 1991
Franklin Watts Inc.
387 Park Avenue South
New York, NY 10016

ISBN 0-531-10710-8 (lib.)/ISBN 0-531-24605-1 (pbk.)

Library of Congress Catalog Card Number: 88-51609

Illustrations: Marion Appleton, Howard Dyke, David Mallott,
Charles Raymond

Photographs: Christian Bonnington 45. Health Education Authority
33: Superman is the trade mark of DC Comics Inc. © 1982. Used by
the Health Education Authority under licence. All rights reserved.
Science Photo Library 24. Science Photo Library: CNRI 7, 11, 27;
Martin Dohrn 1, 23; Dr George Gornacz 43; Eric Grave 20; Harvey
Pincis 35; Dr Gary Settles 29; James Stevenson 31. Zefa Picture
Library 13, 19, 30, 39, 40.

All illustrations are from the original edition

Printed in Belgium

Contents

The breath of life

Every few seconds, throughout life, we breathe. We hardly ever think about this seemingly simple act, except perhaps when gasping for breath after strenuous exercise, or when coughing and wheezing during a cold. Yet breathing is vital for life. If the human body does not breathe for a couple of minutes, harm begins to occur. After three or four minutes, the brain starts to suffer irreversible damage. If breathing still fails, death follows.

Why is breathing so important? The reason is based on the need of every **cell** in the body for **oxygen**, a colorless gas in the air. We breathe to take oxygen from the air into the body. Inside each cell, the oxygen is used in biochemical reactions which turn the "fuel" in digested food into a readily available form of energy. This energy can then be used to power thousands of other biochemical processes inside cells – processes which keep us alive.

The parts of the body involved in breathing are called the **respiratory system**. The largest parts of the system are the two **lungs**, which lie in the chest, well protected by the ribs. Besides obtaining oxygen, the respiratory system carries out other functions. It gets rid of **carbon dioxide**, a waste product of cell biochemistry. If carbon dioxide were allowed to build up, it would poison the body. Air passing into the system travels through the nose, allowing us to smell and through the mouth, helping us to taste, and air coming out of the system allows us to make the sounds of speech.

▷ The main parts of the respiratory system are the nostrils and the nasal cavity, the mouth, throat (**pharynx** and **larynx**), **windpipe** (**trachea**), the two lungs with their various airways and the muscular **diaphragm**. The respiratory system absorbs oxygen from air that is breathed in, passing it into the blood. Then the circulatory system, consisting of the heart and blood vessels, distributes this oxygen by pumping and carrying the blood around the body. At the same time, the circulatory system collects waste carbon dioxide and brings it to the lungs, where it is breathed out of the respiratory system into the air.

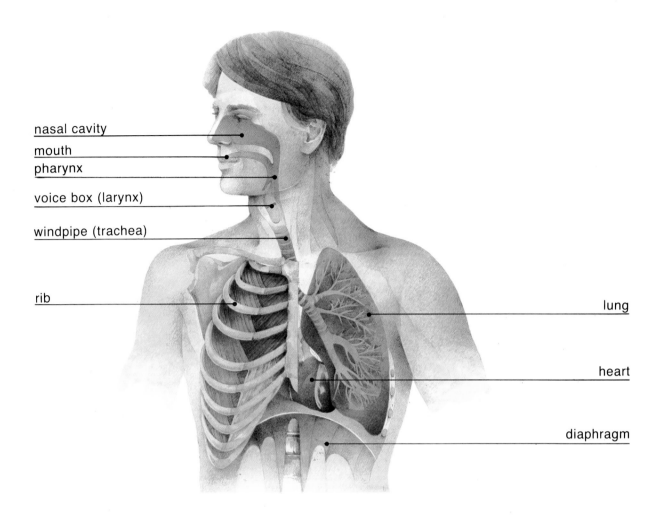

nasal cavity
mouth
pharynx
voice box (larynx)
windpipe (trachea)
rib
lung
heart
diaphragm

The breath of life

- We breathe in air, which is a mixture of gases. Air is about 78% nitrogen, 21% oxygen, 1% argon, 0.03% carbon dioxide and even smaller amounts of other gases. We need only the oxygen in the air.
- The air we breathe out contains less oxygen (about 16%) whilst its carbon dioxide content goes up to nearly 4%.
- A new baby takes about 40 breaths each minute.
- A one-year-old baby takes about 24 breaths each minute.
- On average, an adult takes about fourteen breathing each minute.
- After exercise, such as running a race, the breathing rate can increase to more than 100 breaths per minute.
- Each minute an adult breathes in (and out) some 15–21 pints (7–10 liters) of air. Going in, this air contains nearly 4 pints (2 liters) of oxygen; coming out, it carries 3 pints (1.5 liters) of carbon dioxide.
- Each day an adult takes in around 530 cu ft (15 cu m) of air.
- Each year, an adult breathes in oxygen weighing 275,000 tons.
- In an average lifetime, an adult takes 500 million breaths. This represents 14 million cu ft (400,000 cu m) of air, enough to fill a good-sized oil tanker.

The lungs and chest

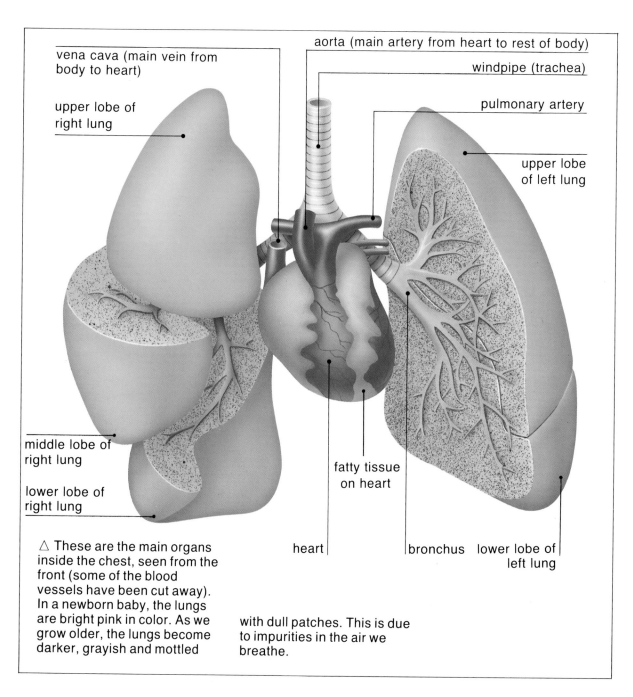

vena cava (main vein from body to heart)

upper lobe of right lung

aorta (main artery from heart to rest of body)

windpipe (trachea)

pulmonary artery

upper lobe of left lung

middle lobe of right lung

lower lobe of right lung

fatty tissue on heart

heart

bronchus

lower lobe of left lung

△ These are the main organs inside the chest, seen from the front (some of the blood vessels have been cut away). In a newborn baby, the lungs are bright pink in color. As we grow older, the lungs become darker, grayish and mottled with dull patches. This is due to impurities in the air we breathe.

The two lungs almost fill the chest, and look like two large, pinkish, cone-shaped sponges. When filled with air they may weigh just over 2 lb (1 kg) in an adult – they are so light because they contain much air.

The lungs are not quite the same size. The right lung is slightly larger than the left lung. This is partly because the heart, which fits snugly between the lungs, lies mainly in a hollow in the inner side of the left lung. The right lung is divided into three main sections (lobes), whilst the left lung has two lobes.

The chest contains several other organs besides the lungs and heart. There are the main **arteries** leading from the heart to the rest of the body. There are the main **veins**, bringing blood from the body back to the heart, and there are the short arteries and veins which connect the lungs to the heart. The chest also contains the main airway, the windpipe (trachea), to the lungs. This divides into two smaller airways called the **bronchi**. One bronchus goes to each lung.

The organs in the chest are always moving. About once every second, the heart pumps (beats) and its muscular walls squeeze blood out along the arteries. The arteries pulse with the pressure of each heartbeat. About once every four seconds, the lungs expand and contract as we breathe in and out. The movements of the lungs are well lubricated by thin, slippery membranes, called **pleurae**. Each lung is covered by one pleura, which is folded around its lobes and airways. The pleura is also folded around and back on itself, to line the inside of the chest around that lung. In addition, the heart has a smooth, slippery covering, called the pericardium, which allows it to move easily within the chest.

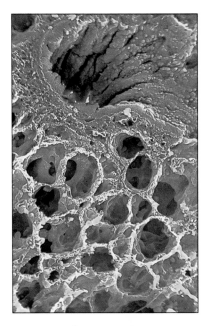

△ The spongy, air-filled nature of the lungs can be seen in this microscope photograph. The lung tissue has been cut through to show one of the small airways, called a **bronchiole** (the tunnel near the top). The circles in the lower half of the photograph are the tiny bubble-like air sacs called **alveoli**. The yellow areas are the tissue which connects and supports the alveoli.

The nose and mouth

The entrances and exits to the respiratory system are the nose and, to some extent, the mouth. The mouth and the nasal cavity (behind the nose) are separated by the **palate**. This forms the roof of the mouth and the floor of the nasal cavity. The palate has two parts. At the front is the hard palate, which is a rigid shelf of bone. At the back is the soft palate, a flexible flap of muscular and connective tissue.

Normally we breathe through the nose, which is specially equipped to change the incoming air. Hairs in the nostrils filter out unwanted particles, such as dust. Some particles stick to the **mucous membrane** which lines the nasal cavity. The nose and nasal cavity have a good supply of blood, which warms the incoming air. Water evaporates from the cavity lining and moisturizes the air. In this way the lungs receive filtered, warmed, humidified air, which allows them to work more effectively.

We may breathe through the mouth after vigorous activity, since we can take more air into the system this way. Some people, when asleep, breathe in partly through the mouth and the air rattles the soft palate, causing the noise we call snoring.

Inside the nasal cavity are thin ledges of bone called **turbinates** or **nasal conchae**. These channel the air backward but allow some air to circulate near the organs of smell in the roof of the nasal cavity. These organs detect airborne odor molecules and send nerve signals to the brain.

▷ This cut-away view shows that there are two large cavities directly behind the outer surface of the face. These are the nasal cavity and the mouth. The many jobs carried out by the nose and mouth are shown along the top of the diagram.

8

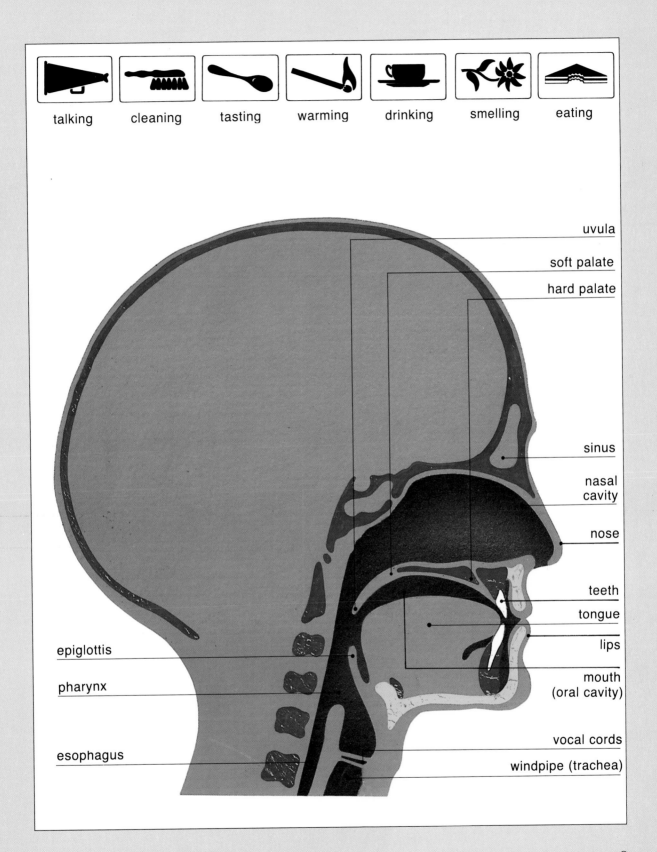

talking   cleaning   tasting   warming   drinking   smelling   eating

uvula

soft palate

hard palate

sinus

nasal cavity

nose

teeth

tongue

lips

mouth (oral cavity)

vocal cords

windpipe (trachea)

epiglottis

pharynx

esophagus

9

The bronchial tree

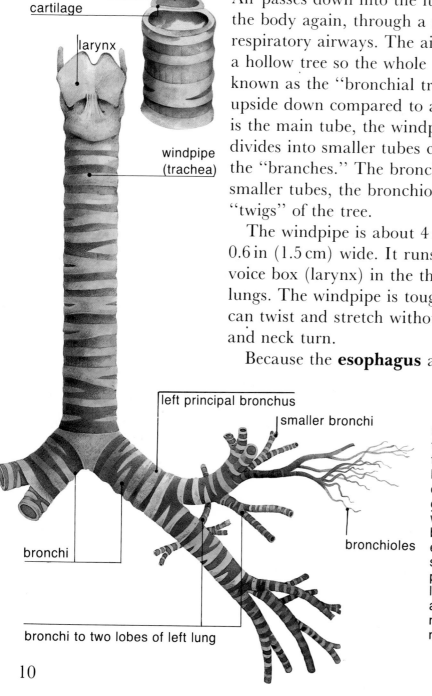

esophagus

cartilage

larynx

windpipe (trachea)

left principal bronchus

smaller bronchi

bronchi

bronchioles

bronchi to two lobes of left lung

Air passes down into the lungs and back up, out of the body again, through a series of tubes, the respiratory airways. The airways branch rather like a hollow tree so the whole branching system is known as the "bronchial tree" – although it is upside down compared to a real tree! The "trunk" is the main tube, the windpipe (trachea). This divides into smaller tubes called bronchi, which are the "branches." The bronchi divide in turn into smaller tubes, the bronchioles, which are the "twigs" of the tree.

The windpipe is about 4 in (10 cm) long and 0.6 in (1.5 cm) wide. It runs from the bottom of the voice box (larynx) in the throat down between the lungs. The windpipe is tough and flexible, so that it can twist and stretch without kinking as the head and neck turn.

Because the **esophagus** and the lungs press on

◁ The respiratory airways resemble an upside-down tree. Hoops of cartilage stiffen the windpipe and larger bronchi. This keeps them open, even where the esophagus presses on the windpipe (above left). Each bronchus divides about eighteen times, becoming smaller and smaller, whilst the pieces of cartilage become less common. The smallest airways, the bronchioles, have no cartilage. Their walls are made of strands of muscle.

10

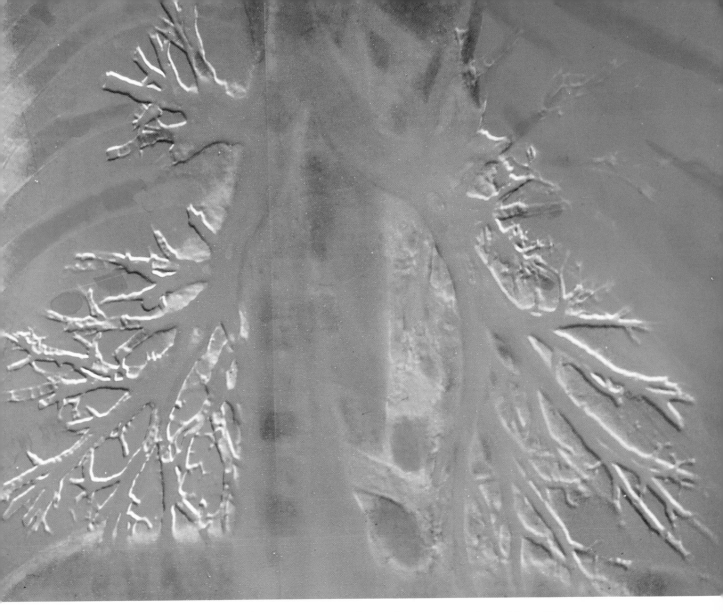

the windpipe, it must be kept open so that air can flow back and forth freely. About sixteen to twenty stiff, C-shaped pieces of **cartilage** are built into its walls to hold it open.

The windpipe branches into two main bronchi; the left one is about 2 in (5 cm) long and the right one is 1 in (2.5 cm) long. These divide further, into bronchi that go to each lobe of each lung. The branching continues until the airways become bronchioles, the smallest of which are only 0.04 in (1 mm) across. The whole of the bronchial tree is lined with mucous membrane, which helps to keep the system clean (see page 26).

△ In this artificially-colored X-ray photograph, the lung tissue appears blue, the ribs are green and the airways are red. The windpipe divides near the top of the photograph. Running down the center is the backbone (spine) and the shadowy line of the esophagus. At the base, in red, is the diaphragm, the sheet-like muscle across the base of the chest (see page 12).

11

The muscular diaphragm

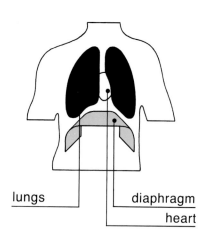

lungs   diaphragm

heart

△ The domed diaphragm forms the floor of the chest, with the lungs and heart sitting on top of it. The upper abdominal organs, such as the liver and stomach, stick up into the underside of the dome. In this diagram, the diaphragm is relaxed. When it contracts, it pulls down and becomes flatter.

The main part of the body, called the torso, is divided into the chest (thorax), the upper part, and the abdomen, which is the lower part.

The organs in the two parts carry out different functions. The organs in the chest are concerned with breathing and circulation. The abdominal organs are involved in digestion, excretion and reproduction. A bell-shaped sheet of muscle called the diaphragm, separates the chest from the abdomen. The edges of the diaphragm are connected to the base of the breastbone (**sternum**), the lower borders of the rib cage and the spine. It curves upward in the center and tough straps of tissue called **ligaments** help to keep it in place and prevent over-stretching.

The diaphragm has three main holes in it. One is for the esophagus, which passes down through the chest to the stomach. Another is for the **aorta**, the main artery from the heart which carries blood to the lower body. The third is for the inferior **vena cava**, the main vein which returns blood from the lower body back to the heart.

Because it is a muscle, the diaphragm can shorten (contract). As it does so, it becomes flatter and makes the chest cavity bigger. This pulls the lungs down, making them enlarge and suck in air. When the diaphragm relaxes, it springs back into its bell-like, domed shape, the chest becomes smaller and air is pushed out of the lungs. These movements are the basis of normal, quiet breathing (see page 16).

△ This jazz horn-player from New Orleans uses his diaphragm to help control his breathing, and so his playing. Musicians sometimes call jazz playing "blowing," which is quite an accurate term!

The benefits of good breathing

Breath control helps the body in various ways. The diaphragm's normal breathing movements happen automatically. But we can also control this muscle at will to regulate our breathing

● **Acting and singing**
Breath control is important in order to speak or sing at the right volume, to hit the right notes, and to project the voice.

● **Breathing and exercise**
Deep breathing before activity helps to flush out carbon dioxide and obtain more oxygen. Extra-deep breathing is called hyperventilation.

● **Relaxation and stress**
Breathing exercises can help to relax the body, improve posture and rest and clear the mind. They are used in yoga and meditation.

The flexible rib cage

The vital organs inside the chest are well protected by the bony cage formed by the ribs, the breastbone (sternum) and the spine.

There are twelve pairs of ribs. They are springy, arch-shaped bones which curve around the sides of the chest. At the back, each pair is joined to one of the bones called vertebrae, which make up the spine. At the front, the upper seven pairs of ribs are joined to the breastbone via strips of flexible cartilage, the costal cartilages. The eighth to tenth pairs of ribs join on to the cartilages of the pair above.

▷ The ribs, breastbone and spine form a strong yet flexible cage, which moves to allow breathing to take place. The ribs are unusually springy for bones. When knocked, they are more likely to bend and absorb the force, rather than crack or splinter, and puncture the lungs – a life-threatening injury.

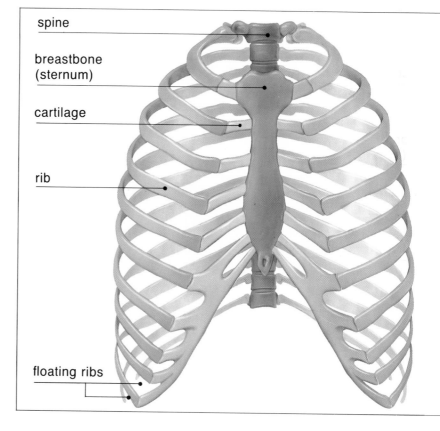

spine

breastbone (sternum)

cartilage

rib

floating ribs

The last two pairs of ribs are shorter and do not join at the front. They are known as floating ribs. The ends of the floating ribs are buried in the muscles of the wall of the chest.

The joints between the ribs, spine and breastbone are movable, which means that the whole rib cage can move. **Intercostal muscles** run between each pair of ribs and other muscles connect the ribs to the breastbone and the spine. When these muscles contract, they lift the ribs so that the front of the rib cage swings upward and outward. This makes the chest cavity bigger, enlarges the lungs and sucks in air. (At the same time the diaphragm moves down and also enlarges the chest cavity, which expands the lungs even more.) When the muscles relax, the front of the rib cage falls down and in again and air is pushed out of the lungs.

▽ Muscles in, around and above the rib cage help to carry out breathing movements. The intercostal muscles connect one pair of ribs with the next. The scalene muscles run from the top two pairs of ribs up to the neck. When the muscles are relaxed, the rib cage is relatively flat and narrow. As the muscles contract, the cage moves upward and outward ....

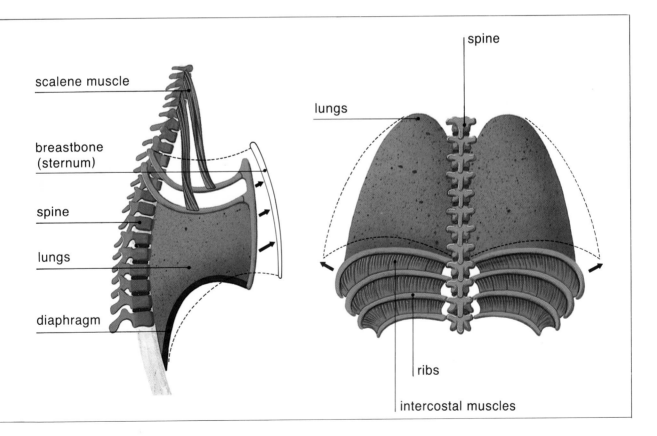

scalene muscle

breastbone (sternum)

spine

lungs

diaphragm

spine

lungs

ribs

intercostal muscles

Breathing in and out

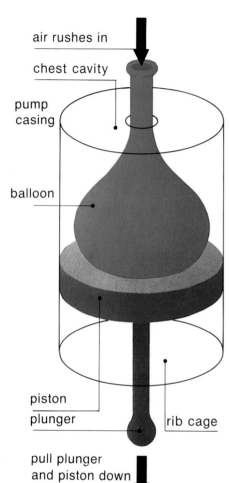

air rushes in

chest cavity

pump casing

balloon

piston

plunger

rib cage

pull plunger and piston down

△ The lungs work like a bellows pump. In this model, the lungs are represented by a balloon, which is an airtight fit in its casing (the chest). The diaphragm is a piston and plunger. When the piston is pulled down, the balloon expands and low air pressure is created inside it. Air is sucked in through its neck – the windpipe.

Stand sideways in front of a mirror and breathe very gently. There are hardly any movements to be seen. In normal, quiet breathing the diaphragm does most of the work. As the diaphragm contracts, its center moves down about 0.6 in (1.5 cm) and presses on the abdomen, squashing it outward.

For deep breathing, other muscles go to work. Muscles in the chest, back and neck pull the ribs up and out, to suck more air into the lungs. When you breathe out, the abdominal muscles stiffen so the diaphragm is forced higher into the chest, pushing out more air.

With each normal breath, you do not change all the air in the lungs. Only a proportion, the tidal volume, flows in and out. You breathe in about 6 pints (3 liters) of air and breathe out about 2 pints (1 liter) of air.

The lungs play no active part in breathing. They simply expand and contract as the rib cage moves. It is rather like squeezing a bath sponge in your hand. The muscles in your hand do the work and the sponge, like the lungs, changes shape passively. In fact, the lungs are stretched rather than squeezed from their normal shape. Their outer surfaces stay in contact with the lining of the chest so that, as the chest cavity enlarges, the lungs are pulled outward. (It is as though your fingers were stuck to the sponge and, as you opened them, the sponge stretched.) This movement creates low air pressure inside the lungs. Air rushes in to equalize the pressure – and you breathe in.

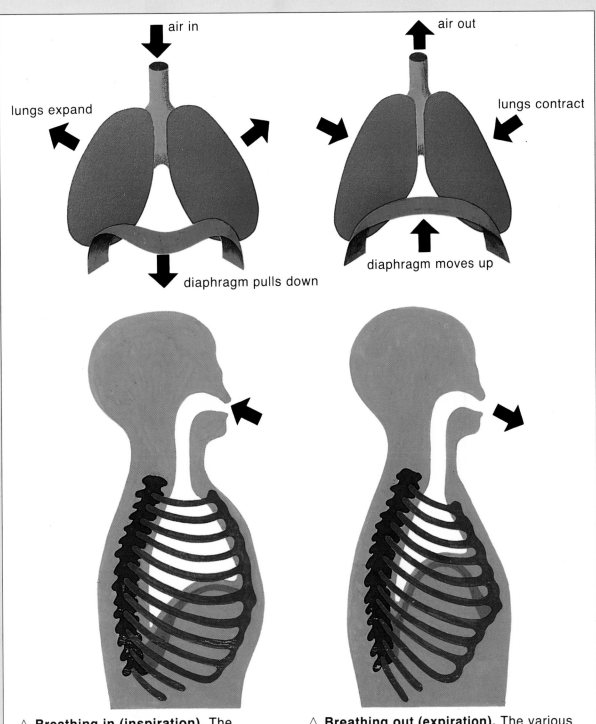

air in

lungs expand

diaphragm pulls down

air out

lungs contract

diaphragm moves up

△ **Breathing in (inspiration).** The diaphragm (red) flattens, whilst the ribs and breastbone swivel up and out on their hinge-like joints. The space for the lungs (white in the lower diagram) becomes bigger.

△ **Breathing out (expiration).** The various muscles relax. The natural elastic recoil of the lungs makes them spring back to their smaller size, aided by gravity which pulls down and flattens the rib cage.

The brain coordinates breathing

You do not have to remember to breathe. It is an automatic process, like the heart beating. It happens whether you are concentrating hard, daydreaming, asleep, or even unconscious.

However, the chest and lungs do not breathe on their own. They need to be coordinated with other body processes. For example, when your muscles are very active, you must breathe harder to supply them with more oxygen. This coordination is carried out through the control center of the body – the brain.

The breathing control center or respiratory center

▽ Control of breathing is mainly chemical. Sensors around the body detect the levels of carbon dioxide and oxygen. They feed this information to the brain's respiratory center. As the carbon dioxide level rises, and the oxygen level falls, breathing becomes harder and faster.

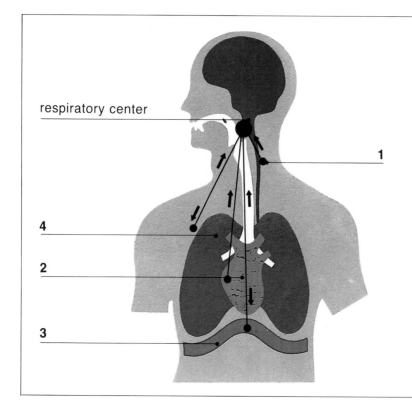

respiratory center

1

4

2

3

The respiratory center is the coordination point for control of breathing. The center receives signals from brain stem cells and sensors in the aorta (main artery) about the level of carbon dioxide in the body.
1 Sensors in the carotid artery also send signals about levels of carbon dioxide and oxygen to the respiratory center. The center even receives signals from stretch sensors in the chest muscles and the lungs themselves
2 Nerve signals are sent out to the diaphragm
3 and chest muscles
4 to control their contractions and regulate the pattern of breathing.

is in the brain stem. ("**Respiration**" is a term sometimes used to mean breathing, see page 25.) To govern the depth and rate of breathing, the respiratory center sends electrical signals along nerves to the diaphragm and chest muscles. The center acts on information it receives from various sensors in the body. During exercise, the body's muscles produce more carbon dioxide, which builds up in the blood. The carbon dioxide level is detected by sensor cells in the brain stem and other sites in the body. As muscles work, they also use up oxygen. The oxygen level in the blood is detected by sensor cells, for example, in the carotid artery of the neck.

A lifesaving reaction is built into the system. You can only hold your breath for a short time before the body's automatic response takes over and you have to take deep breaths once again.

△ Breathing is finely tuned to the amount of fresh oxygen the body needs and the amount of carbon dioxide it must get rid of. When we sleep, most muscles rest. Less carbon dioxide is produced and less oxygen is required, so breathing is slower and more shallow than when we are awake.

Exchange in the lungs

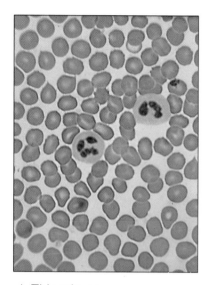

△ This microscope photograph shows many red blood cells, the body's oxygen-carriers. There are more than five million red blood cells in a tiny drop of blood. They give blood its red color. Also in the photograph are two large white blood cells, which help the body to fight off disease.

Throughout the lungs, there are many 1,000s of tiny bronchioles. At the end of each bronchiole, like a bunch of grapes hanging on a stalk, is a cluster of bubble-shaped air cells called alveoli. The walls of the alveoli are only one cell thick. Around each alveolus is a network of **capillaries**, the smallest blood vessels in the body. The walls of the capillaries are only one cell thick too. So the air in the alveoli is only two cells away from the blood around it.

Oxygen in the air inside the alveoli is more concentrated than in the blood, so oxygen passes from the air into the blood. But for carbon dioxide, the reverse is true, so carbon dioxide passes from the blood into the air. One gas is exchanged for the other and so the process is called "**gas exchange**." Each portion of blood has only one-quarter of a second to exchange gases as it flows past the alveoli.

Although each alveolus is microscopic, its spherical shape provides a relatively large surface area for gas exchange. And there are more than 500 million alveoli in the two lungs together. So the total area for gas exchange is enormous. If all the alveoli were flattened out, they would cover around 96 sq yd (80 sq m) – over 2,000 pages like this one.

Red blood cells contain a special chemical, **hemoglobin**, which strongly attracts oxygen molecules and links to them to form **oxyhemoglobin**. This chemical carries oxygen around the body.

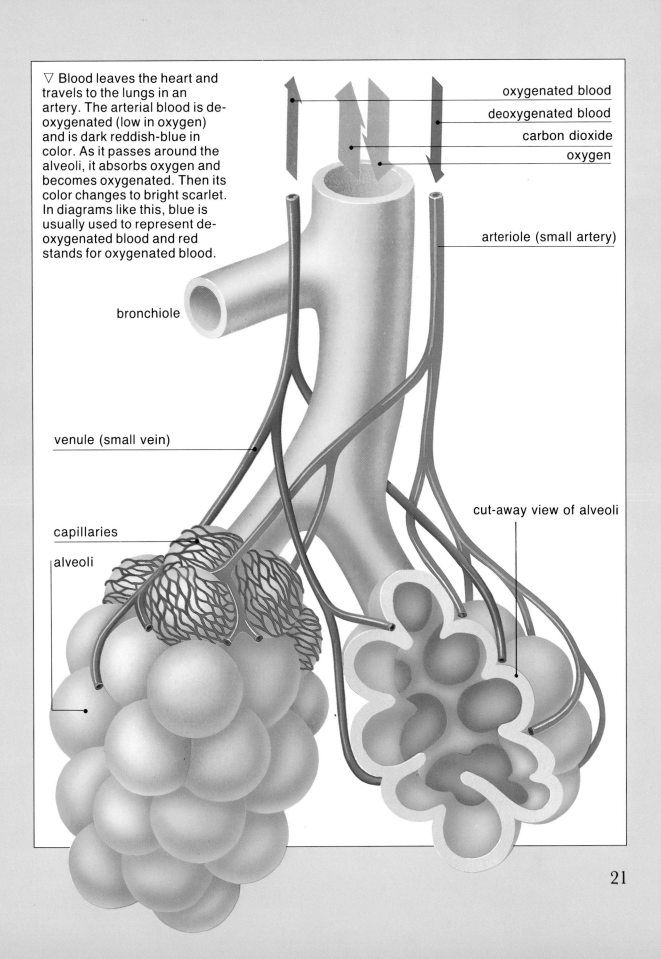

▽ Blood leaves the heart and travels to the lungs in an artery. The arterial blood is de-oxygenated (low in oxygen) and is dark reddish-blue in color. As it passes around the alveoli, it absorbs oxygen and becomes oxygenated. Then its color changes to bright scarlet. In diagrams like this, blue is usually used to represent de-oxygenated blood and red stands for oxygenated blood.

oxygenated blood

deoxygenated blood

carbon dioxide

oxygen

arteriole (small artery)

bronchiole

venule (small vein)

cut-away view of alveoli

capillaries

alveoli

Double circulation

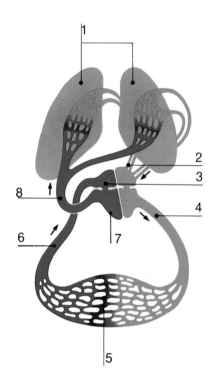

△ This diagram shows the double circulation, which is like a figure eight with the heart at the cross over. The part through the lungs is the pulmonary circulation; that through the body tissues is the systemic circulation.

1 Lungs
2 Pulmonary veins
3 Left side of heart
4 Aorta
5 Body tissues
6 Main veins
7 Right side of heart
8 Pulmonary artery
Red: oxygenated blood
Blue: de- oxygenated blood

Blood flows continuously through the lungs, picking up fresh supplies of oxygen. But after passing through the lung capillaries, it is at very low pressure and does not have enough driving force to carry on all around the body. So it returns to the heart, which pushes it on its journey to deliver its oxygen to all body tissues.

If oxygenated blood were to mix with de-oxygenated blood in the heart, the vital oxygen would not be distributed so efficiently. To avoid this, there is a double circulation. The heart is not one pump but two, side by side, in the one organ. The smaller pump on the right side sends blood along the short **pulmonary artery** to the lungs. This blood is de-oxygenated and dark reddish-blue. When it leaves the lungs along the **pulmonary veins**, it is freshly oxygenated and bright reddish-scarlet.

The oxygenated blood arrives back at the heart's left pump. This has a thicker wall and is more powerful than the right pump. It forces blood out along the body's main artery, the aorta, which divides and carries the blood to all parts of the body. In the tissues, blood unloads its oxygen and picks up carbon dioxide, turning dark-reddish blue in the process.

The de-oxygenated blood flows back to the right pump of the heart again through the main veins, the venae cavae. It then begins the whole journey again, going around and around in a two part, never ending cycle. It takes about one minute to complete each cycle.

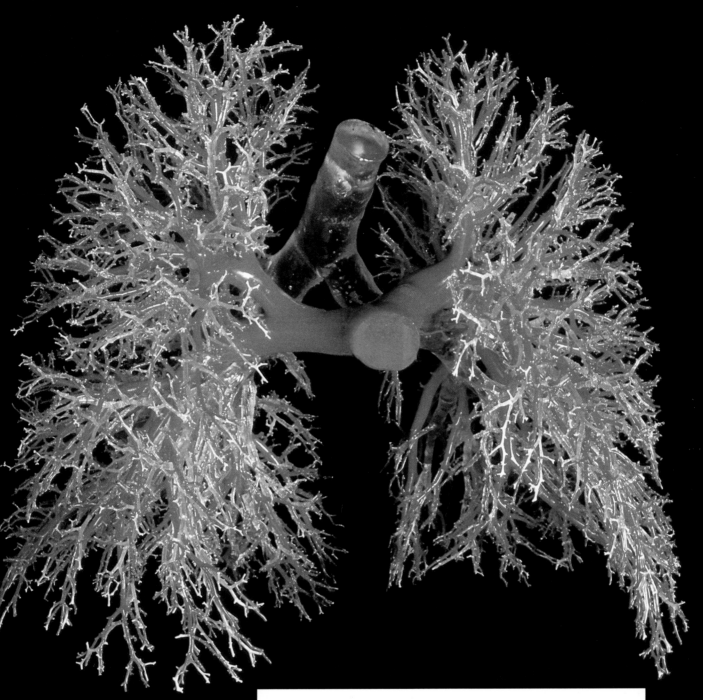

△ This is a cast of the lung's airways and blood vessels. It is made by filling the passages with a resin-type material that hardens when it sets, and then dissolving away the tissues. The airways are in yellow, with the lower windpipe and main bronchi in the upper center. The pulmonary artery and its branches are in red. (The third network, the pulmonary veins, is not shown.)

The great tissue exchange

△ The peak flow meter is a device which measures the flow of air from the lungs – in other words, the fastest rate at which you can breathe out. It is a useful test for illnesses like **asthma** and **bronchitis**, which involve breathing problems. It is also a rough guide to general fitness.

Fresh blood, loaded with oxygen and nutrients, leaves the left side of the heart and travels along arteries, which branch and become smaller and smaller. Eventually they become microscopic blood vessels called capillaries, which penetrate almost every part of the body. Nearly all the oxygen is transported in the form of oxyhemoglobin, the red substance in red blood cells. The nutrients travel in solution, dissolved in the watery part of the blood, the **plasma**.

The only regions of the body which do not have a network of capillaries are dead tissues, such as the hair, the nails and the surface of the skin, and certain parts of the eye, where blood would interfere with clear vision.

Fresh, oxygenated blood arriving in the capillaries contains more oxygen and nutrients than the surrounding tissues. So the molecules of oxygen and nutrients pass through the one-cell-thin capillary walls into the tissues, in order to equalize the levels.

The reverse happens with carbon dioxide and other waste products of biochemical reactions. These are at high levels in the tissues but low levels in newly-arrived blood. So these substances pass from the tissues into the blood. Some carbon dioxide leaves the tissues dissolved in the plasma, whilst some travels (like oxygen) in red blood cells.

When the "great exchange" has taken place, the blood flows on into veins and eventually back to the right side of the heart.

Aerobic and anaerobic respiration

"Respiration" is sometimes used to describe breathing (see page 16). It is also the name for the chain of biochemical reactions in cells, which release energy from nutrients.

- Aerobic respiration uses oxygen from red blood cells, (supplied via the lungs), to produce energy in the body's cells. Aerobic exercises include swimming, cycling and jogging, which make your lungs and heart work harder to supply enough oxygen.
- Anaerobic respiration occurs during short bursts of activity, such as sprinting or weightlifting. The muscles use so much oxygen so quickly that they must rely on a different biochemical pathway. This causes wastes like lactic acid to build up in the muscles.

▽ A dense network of capillaries winds around the tiny fibers which make up a muscle, bringing the blood which supplies oxygen and energy. A hard-working muscle may use up to 50 times more oxygen than it does when resting.

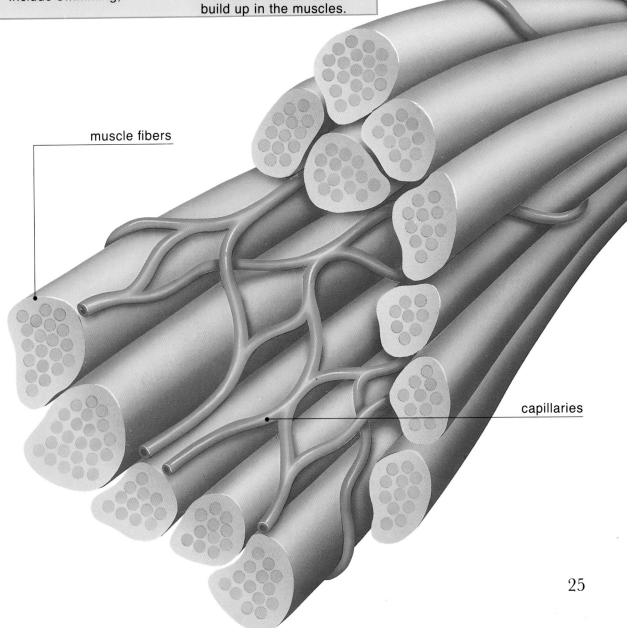

muscle fibers

capillaries

25

Filtered airways

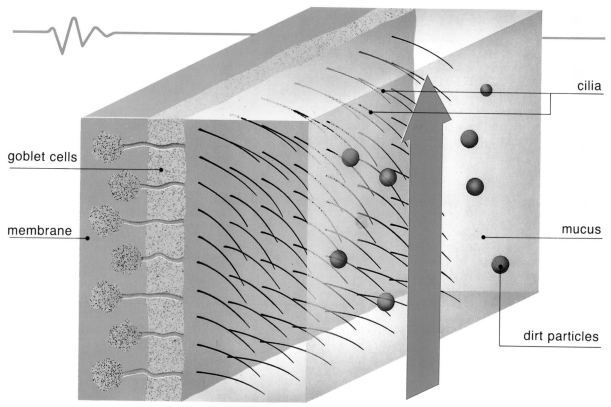

cilia

goblet cells

membrane

mucus

dirt particles

△ This diagram shows a much-enlarged portion of the wall of an airway, such as a bronchus. Goblet cells make a layer of sticky mucus which covers the inner lining of the airway. The hair-like cilia are about to bend in the direction of the arrow, "rowing" the layer of mucus and dirt up and out of the lungs.

Tiny floating particles of dust and other substances are breathed deep into the lungs. If they were allowed to collect, they would soon clog the airways and damage the alveoli. The lungs, however, continually clean themselves.

The first cleaning method involves **mucus**, a sticky fluid, and **cilia**, microscopic hair-like structures. The mucus is made continuously by special cells called **goblet cells**, in the lining of the airways. The mucus coats the lining as a thin layer and traps any particles which settle on it.

The mucus is not motionless. The tiny cilia stick out from the surface of the lining and wave back and forth with a coordinated beating motion, like a field of corn swaying back and forth in the wind. They propel the mucus along the airways and out

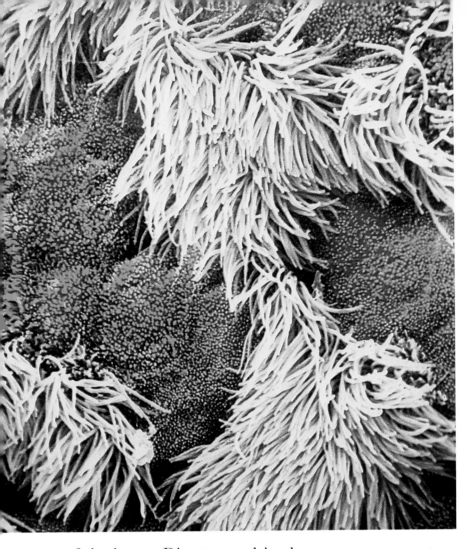

◁ In this colored microscope photograph, the cilia are magnified about 10,000 times; they look like patches of yellow corn and one interspersed with goblet cells.

Air pollution

The air we breathe is not clean and pure. It has been polluted by all kinds of substances:

- Carbon monoxide, mainly from the fumes of vehicle exhausts and factories.
- Sulfur dioxide, and other sulfur oxides, mainly from the fumes of power stations.
- Nitrogen oxides, from industrial chimneys and vehicle exhausts.
- Smog (a combination of the words smoke and fog) may be produced when water vapor in the air condenses on dust particles from industrial smoke.
- Photochemical smog forms when sunlight shines on various chemicals in the air, mainly those from vehicle exhaust fumes.
- Scientists estimate that a person living in a large industrial city breathes in up to 20,000 million tiny particles of dust and other foreign matter, every day.
- New York City suffered a "killer smog" in 1966.
- The "pea-soup" fog in London in 1952 contributed to nearly 4,000 deaths in one week.

of the lungs. Dirt trapped in the mucus moves at a speed of about 0.4 in (1 cm) each minute and flows up the windpipe to the throat. Every so often we harmlessly swallow the mucus, perhaps with a cough – we call this "clearing the throat."

The second cleaning method involves white cells called **macrophages** in the alveoli. The macrophages wrap their jelly-like bodies around any particles, "swallowing" and digesting them.

With almost every breath, we take in disease-causing germs, like viruses and **bacteria**. If there are too many germs for the mucus or macrophages to deal with, or if the lungs are weak or damaged in some way, the germs take hold. We may then suffer from a respiratory infection such as pneumonia or bronchitis.

Coughing and sneezing

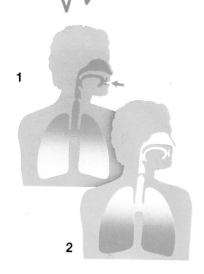

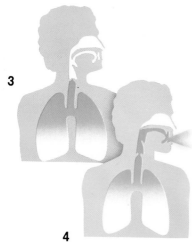

△ A cough happens in four main stages:
1 Air is breathed in deeply.
2 The vocal cords in the throat close, to seal off the airways.
3 The chest muscles and diaphragm contract and squeeze the air in the lungs, increasing air pressure.
4 The vocal cords relax, the air suddenly expands and shoots out through the mouth.

The respiratory system has two main ways of clearing blockages – coughing and sneezing. They both happen automatically. A cough is caused by something irritating the lining of the lower respiratory airways.

After a deep breath, the **vocal cords** in the voice box (larynx) of the throat close together to make an airtight seal. The diaphragm and chest muscles contract to compress the air in the lungs and airways. Then the vocal cords relax, suddenly releasing the air pressure. Air rushes from the lungs up through the throat and mouth, rattling the cords and causing the noise of the cough. This sudden "gale" of air blows through the windpipe at speeds of over 300 mph (500 kph), sweeping away any obstruction in its path. Coughed-up mucus and other material is usually swallowed.

A sneeze is a response to irritation of the lining in the nose or nasal cavity. The basic process is the same as for a cough, but in this case the soft palate blocks the back of the nasal cavity. When air is released, it shoots out through the nose at speeds of over 90 mph (150 kph). A single sneeze may spray as many as 100,000 droplets of mucus and germs into the air.

Hiccups are occasional, uncontrolled contractions of the diaphragm. Why they begin is something of a mystery. It may be that the stomach is over-stretched after a large meal or too much drink. This irritates the diaphragm and the nerve which controls it, sending it out of control.

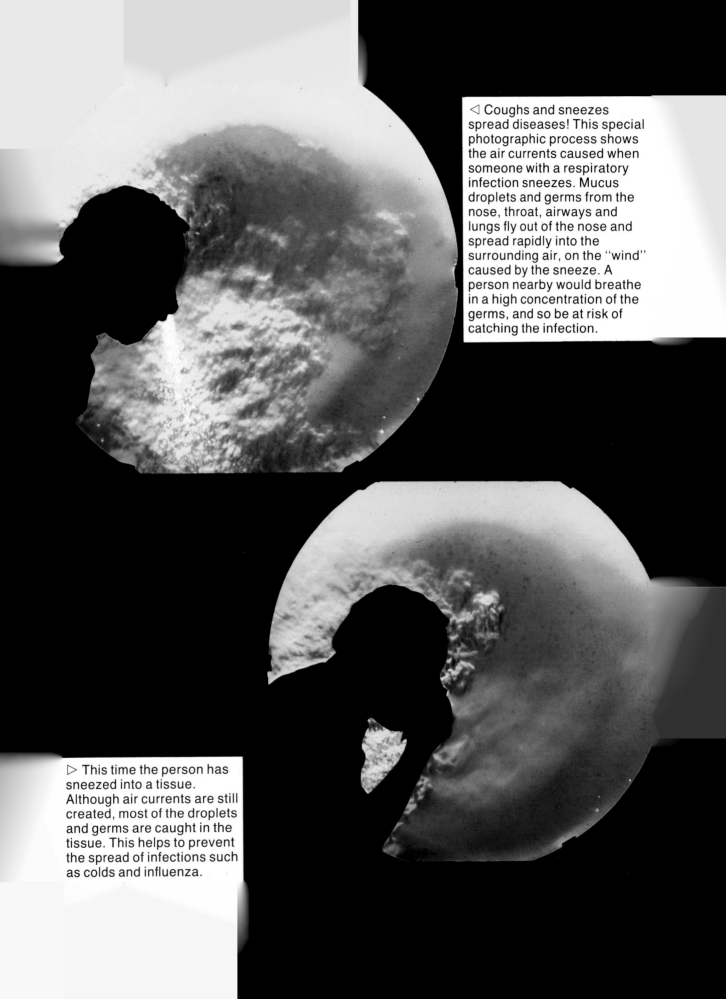

◁ Coughs and sneezes spread diseases! This special photographic process shows the air currents caused when someone with a respiratory infection sneezes. Mucus droplets and germs from the nose, throat, airways and lungs fly out of the nose and spread rapidly into the surrounding air, on the "wind" caused by the sneeze. A person nearby would breathe in a high concentration of the germs, and so be at risk of catching the infection.

▷ This time the person has sneezed into a tissue. Although air currents are still created, most of the droplets and germs are caught in the tissue. This helps to prevent the spread of infections such as colds and influenza.

Smoking devastates the body

Dangers to others

Some people argue that if they want to smoke and harm themselves, that's their business. But people who smoke may harm others, too.

- Passive, involuntary or secondary smoking means breathing in other people's tobacco smoke. This can possibly cause illness. Children who live in a house where adults smoke have more respiratory problems.
- A woman who smokes during pregnancy can cause harm to her baby. The baby is more likely to be premature (born early), underweight and have breathing problems.

Smoking involves so many health risks, it is difficult to know where to start. Yet millions of people smoke. Most of them know it harms their bodies, increases their chances of illness and brings death closer. On average, each cigarette takes five minutes off a person's life.

Tobacco smoke contains at least three dangerous substances. One is **nicotine**. This chemical is absorbed by the lungs and acts on the brain and nervous system and consequently some people say smoking makes them feel more relaxed and at ease. A great problem is that nicotine is addictive. This means that once the body gets used to nicotine, it wants a continuous supply of it and reacts badly if the nicotine supply is withdrawn.

The second substance is carbon monoxide. This gas takes the place of oxygen in the blood. Less oxygen is transported to the tissues, with harmful side-effects on the heart, arteries and tissues.

The third substance is tar. It is inhaled as a vapor into the lungs. There it condenses into a thick liquid which clogs the airways, kills the tiny cilia hairs and can possibly trigger cancer.

Smoking affects many parts of the body. Direct effects on the lungs themselves include increased risk of lung cancer, infections such as bronchitis, pneumonia and the lung disease **emphysema**. Other risks include heart attacks, mouth and throat cancer, headaches, strokes and diseases of the stomach, intestines, bladder and reproductive organs.

▷ This photograph shows a slice or cross section through the lungs of a healthy adult. There are a certain number of dark specks, which come from dust and other material breathed in from the air. With today's polluted atmosphere, these sort of lung deposits are almost normal. They have little effect on the efficient working of the lungs.

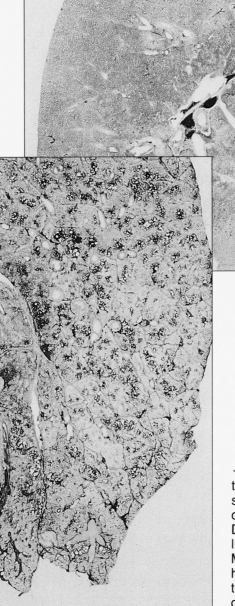

◁ A cross section through the lungs of someone who smoked shows how smoking devastates the lung tissue. Dark, sticky deposits of tar litter the airways and alveoli. Many of the cilia, the tiny hairs which helped to clean the lungs, are dead and gone.

Stop smoking!

The smoker's risks

If you smoke, you run a long list of increased health risks. Compared to non-smokers, people who smoke are:

- Twice as likely to die from heart disease.
- Ten times more likely to develop cancer of the mouth or throat.
- 25 times more likely to develop lung cancer, which is usually fatal.
- More likely to develop colds, coughs, bronchitis and other respiratory disorders.
- More likely to suffer badly and for a longer time from these disorders, rather than recover quickly.
- In the United States, more than 300,000 people die each year from illnesses related to smoking.
- In the United Kingdom, annual deaths from the same cause are around 80,000.
- Millions of people succeed in giving up smoking. About 1 million do so each year in the United States.

Why do people smoke, even when they know of the dangers involved? There are many reasons. Some young people start to smoke because they see adults doing so. They think that smoking will make them seem grown up and mature. Some people say smoking makes them feel more relaxed. Others like to feel part of a group as they share cigarettes and light up with others. Or they may feel awkward if they have nothing to do with their hands.

Knowing why you smoke is the first step in giving it up. It is always worth giving up, even after years of smoking, as, when you stop, the many health risks start to go down. You soon feel more fit and more alert, your senses of smell and taste improve and you feel less breathless.

There are many ways to give up smoking. One of the most effective is simply to stop, all at once, with no preparation and no conditions attached. There may be a short period of after-effects but health then improves rapidly.

Some people gradually reduce the number of cigarettes each day; others collect the money they would have spent on tobacco and buy an occasional treat. Some join a group where they are encouraged to give up smoking by talking to each other and to ex-smokers. It also helps to choose no smoking areas in theaters,. restaurants, trains and planes and to be aware that many people nowadays are against smoking.

There is one sure way to avoid giving up smoking and it is the best way. Never start.

◁ Advertising campaigns against smoking are being aimed at younger people. Some involve well-known personalities, both real and imaginary! The hope is that young people will be persuaded never to start smoking in the first place.

Respiratory illnesses

normal
bronchiole

bronchiole
inflamed
and narrowed
by asthma

 Asthma is a respiratory disorder involving the bronchial airways. The muscle bands around the bronchi and bronchioles contract, narrowing the passageways for air. This causes wheezing and shortage of breath. Asthma tends to occur in sudden attacks, with normal breathing in between. It is sometimes due to an **allergy**, an overreaction of the body's defences to harmless substances, like dust or pollen, in the air.

The respiratory system is one of the most vulnerable parts of the body. Because of the work it does, it is exposed to dirt and germs in the air.

Many respiratory illnesses involve infection by germs. The common cold is caused by types of virus called rhinoviruses. They make the nasal passages inflamed (swollen and sore) and the lining produces much more mucus than usual. **Sinusitis** is inflammation of the linings of the **sinuses** (air-filled cavities in the skull bones) which are linked to the nasal passages. Usually caused by germs, it can bring on headaches, other pain and stuffiness.

Pharyngitis or "sore throat" is inflammation of the pharynx, the upper part of the throat, again usually due to infection by viruses or bacteria. Laryngitis affects the voice box or larynx at the top of the windpipe so that the sufferer becomes hoarse. It may be caused by an infection or by using the voice too much.

Inflammation of the bronchi, the main airways in the lungs, is called bronchitis. Again, it is often due to germs, although it is made far worse by smoking. Pneumonia is the general name for a group of illnesses which inflame and damage lung tissues.

In emphysema, some of the bubble-like alveoli in the lungs become damaged. The sufferer becomes more breathless as the lungs lose some of their oxygen-absorbing surface. This condition may be brought on by strained, over-hard breathing as a result of some other respiratory problem, such as asthma or bronchitis.

△ Asthma is quite common in children. About one child in ten has an occasional mild attack. Many outgrow the condition during their teenage years, although some people develop it during adult life. Asthma cannot be cured. But it can be treated, for example by a drug given in an inhaler (as shown here). A fine spray of the drug is breathed into the lungs, where it acts directly on the narrowed airways and helps their muscles to relax.

Hay fever

The medical name for **hay fever** is seasonal allergic rhinitis. "Seasonal" means it occurs only at certain times of the year, most often in late spring and summer. "Allergic" means it is caused by an allergy. This is an over reaction of the body's germ defense system, which makes some people sensitive to the pollen in the air.

"Rhinitis" means the reaction produces inflammation of the mucous membrane lining the nose and nasal cavity. It causes sneezing and an itchy, runny nose from over-production of mucus. In some cases, the reaction also affects the coverings of the eyes, which itch and water, and the throat, leading to a tickly cough.

The human voice

The sound of the human voice begins in the voice-box (larynx) in the throat. The main "framework" of the larynx is made of several pieces of cartilage, a stiff, gristle-like substance. The largest piece is the thyroid cartilage, which has a bulge at the front. In some people, the bulge can be seen under the skin in the neck and is called the "Adam's apple." The cartilages are held together by ligaments and muscles, both inside and outside the larynx.

Stretched across the center of the larynx are two pearly-white, sharp-edged folds of mucous membrane. These are the vocal cords. Since the larynx is at the top of the windpipe, air passes through the cords with every breath. When we breathe quietly at rest, the vocal cords have a

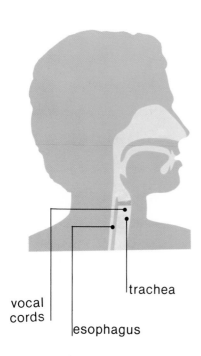

vocal cords | trachea | esophagus

△ The larynx is toward the front of the neck, at the top of the windpipe. It is shaped like an oval tube about 1.6 in (4 cm) long, the same distance from side to side, and 1.2 in (3 cm) from front to back. The vocal cords lie roughly in the middle of the larynx. Each cord is about 0.6 in (1.5 cm) long.

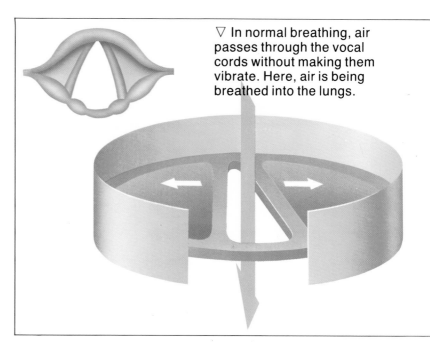

▽ In normal breathing, air passes through the vocal cords without making them vibrate. Here, air is being breathed into the lungs.

triangular gap between them, called the glottis. Air flows through the glottis easily and silently.

There are thirteen muscles in the larynx. When we breathe hard, the muscles act to increase the gap between the vocal cords, allowing more air to pass through. When we wish to speak, the muscles pull the vocal cords almost together. Air passing out of the lungs forces the cords to vibrate (shake back and forth at high speed). This creates the basic sound of the human voice.

If air passes more quickly between the vocal cords, they make more noise and the voice becomes louder. If the vocal cords are stretched more tightly, they vibrate faster and the voice becomes higher.

The airflow from the lungs is slower during speech than during normal breathing. We can speak for many seconds without pausing to draw breath. Some people who have to talk for long periods at a time may become dizzy, since they are not breathing fast enough to obtain sufficient oxygen.

Voice problems

Several disorders can affect the larynx and interfere with speech.

● Laryngitis is an inflammation of the larynx. The sufferer has trouble speaking and the voice may become hoarse (faint and croaky.) It may be due to infection by germs, overuse of the voice, tobacco smoke or drinking alcohol.

● Small lumps may grow in the larynx, on the vocal cords or elsewhere. In some cases these are benign (not cancerous) and can be removed by surgery. In other cases they are cancerous, and if not removed in time, the cancer may spread to other parts of the body.

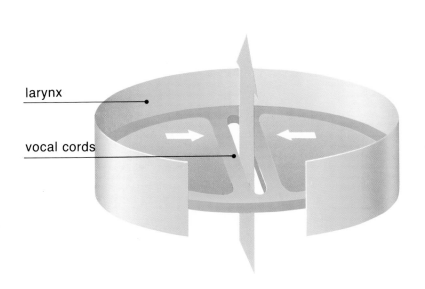

larynx

vocal cords

◁ In speech, the vocal cords are pulled together until there is only a small slit between them. The airstream coming up from the lungs rattles or vibrates the cords, producing the noise we call the voice. The cords are moved by an intricate system of muscles which tilt, twist and pull on the cartilages and ligaments supporting them.

How speech sounds are shaped

The sounds made by the vocal cords in the larynx are, on their own, surprisingly quiet and unvarying. The "shaping" of sounds is carried out by other parts of the respiratory system – the pharynx, hard and soft palates, cheeks, tongue, teeth, lips, nasal cavity and nose. Air in the sinuses also vibrates to amplify the voice (make it louder). During a cold, mucus blocks the nose and sinuses and the voice sounds featureless and flat.

We learn to speak by imitating the sounds of people around us. It requires coordination of dozens of muscles in the throat, neck and face. Stop sounds, such as "p" and "b," are made by suddenly blocking or stopping the flow of air with the lips. Blocking the flow by putting the front of

▽ Try changing from the sound "mmm" to the sound "ahh." All you have to do is open your mouth slightly. The noise made by the larynx, and the position of the tongue and cheeks, remain the same. This shows how altering the pattern of airflow through the head changes the nature of the sound.

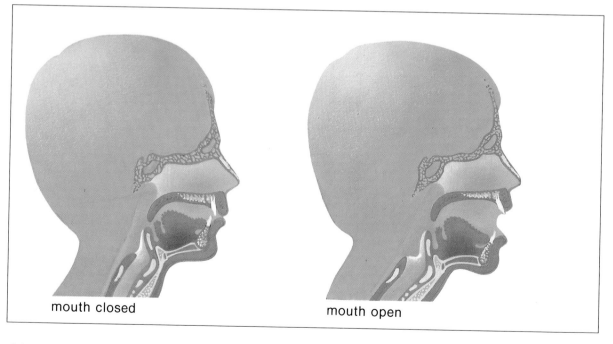

mouth closed

mouth open

the tongue against the hard palate produces "d" or "t" sounds. In "k" and "g" sounds, the back of the tongue blocks against the soft palate.

Fricative sounds are sounds produced by forcing air through a narrowed opening. Examples are "s" and "z," made by using the tongue and hard palate. Vowel sounds, such as "a," "e" and "i," are made by changing the shape of the lips and cheeks, and altering the size of the mouth by lowering the jaw. Nasal sounds, such as "m" and "n," involve closing the mouth, so that the air emerges from the nose.

Another part of the body is vital to speech – the brain. Without the brain to control the speaking muscles, or to interpret the sounds heard by the ears, the finest words would be meaningless.

△ Humans are among the noisiest of all animals. The loudest human scream has been measured at about 110–120 dB (dB stands for decibels, the unit of sound intensity or "loudness"). This compares with about 125 dB for a racing car and over 180 dB for the deep, moaning song of the Blue Whale.

39

The swallowing process

Every time we swallow, a lump of food or a portion of drink is pushed from the back of the mouth down into the pharynx (the upper part of the throat), then into the esophagus and down to the stomach. On the way, it passes 1 cm (0.4 in) or so from the top of the windpipe. The swallowing process must guard against the lump entering the windpipe and causing us to choke and suffocate.

We hardly ever think about swallowing, yet it relies on teams of muscles in the mouth, throat and neck, all working together with precision timing. It is best if food is well chewed before being swallowed. This makes it easier for the tongue to

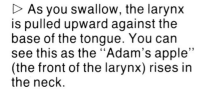

▷ As you swallow, the larynx is pulled upward against the base of the tongue. You can see this as the "Adam's apple" (the front of the larynx) rises in the neck.

mold the food into a lump (bolus) which is moistened with saliva.

The tongue then pushes the food to the back of the mouth, under the flexible flap of the soft palate and along the pharynx. The vocal cords shut and the entire larynx is pulled up against the base of the tongue. Another small flap, the **epiglottis**, seals the entrance to the windpipe. The food slips over the epiglottis and passes on down into the esophagus.

Rarely, a lump of food goes down the wrong way and enters the windpipe instead of the esophagus. If someone who is choking in this way is coughing, they should usually be left alone, since the blasts of air from coughing help to clear the obstruction. Only if the person fails to cough and starts to gasp for air and turn blue, should emergency first aid be given.

▽ We swallow 1,000 times or more during an average day. As well as food and drink, we also swallow saliva and mucus and dirt swept up out of the lungs and airways by their self-cleaning mechanisms.

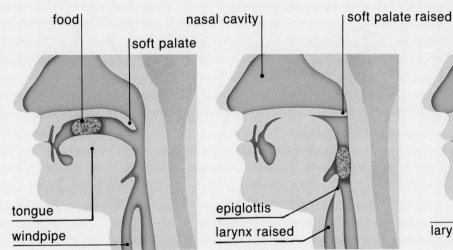

1 In the mouth, food is broken up, chewed into a pulp, mixed with saliva and separated into swallow-sized lumps by the tongue.

2 The soft palate swings up to block the passage into the nasal cavity. The larynx pulls up and the epiglottis folds over its entrance.

3 The food slides over the epiglottis down into the esophagus. Wave-like contractions of the esophagus propel food to the stomach.

Breathing underwater

If we swim underwater, we can hold our breath long enough to stay under for about a minute or so. But for longer dives, we have to take a supply of oxygen with us.

Water is much denser, or "heavier," than air. The deeper a person dives, the greater the pressure on the body from the weight of water above. This squeezes, or compresses, the gas in the lungs. At high pressures, strange things start to happen.

At depths greater than about 130 ft (40 m), the lungs absorb nitrogen from the air inside them. If a diver swims back to the surface quickly, the nitrogen in the blood and tissues reacts by forming bubbles. It is like taking the top off a soda bottle. If you do this too quickly the dissolved gases come out of the solution and bubble over. Nitrogen bubbles in the tissues cause severe pain, especially in the joints. The natural reaction is to bend the joints to try and ease the pain, which is why this disorder, decompression sickness, is sometimes known as "the bends."

Divers who descend to great depths must therefore surface slowly, so that the nitrogen in the body has time to come out of solution and be "blown-off" through the lungs. Or they may come to the surface in a sealed capsule and spend hours, even days, in a pressurized room whilst the pressure is slowly reduced to normal.

To reduce these problems, deep-sea divers breathe special mixtures of gases, such as oxygen and helium.

▷ Divers stay underwater in various ways. "Skin-divers" have no equipment. They simply train until they can hold their breath for several minutes. This is long enough, for example, to collect pearls from oysters on the seabed. Scuba or aqualung divers (shown here), carry tanks of compressed gas on their backs. They breathe the gas through a special pressure valve called a regulator. (Scuba stands for Self-Contained Underwater Breathing Apparatus.) Deep-sea divers wear a special flexible suit and a fiberglass or plastic helmet, with air pumped down a supply line.

Breathing at high altitude

Most human bodies are adapted to life at or around sea level. As we go higher, up a mountain or in a plane, the air becomes less dense or thinner. There is less oxygen in the air, which means we have to breathe harder in order to absorb sufficient supplies. With increasing altitude, the body begins to react against the low pressure and lack of oxygen and suffers from altitude sickness. A person suddenly transported 23,000 ft (7,000 m) high would feel dizzy and begin to lose consciousness after about ten minutes.

In 1875 two French balloonists became the first casualties of sudden altitude sickness. They ascended to over 26,200 ft (8,000 m) but did not have enough oxygen with them. They became so weak that they could not breathe. They perished, although a third balloonist with them survived.

Modern airplanes fly at around 33,000–43,000 ft (10,000–13,000 m), whilst the supersonic Concorde can cruise at 60,000 ft (18,000 m). The planes are sealed and the air inside them is pressurized to the equivalent of about 6,500 ft (2,000 m) altitude. This is hardly noticeable to the passengers, although it may cause the ears to "pop" when the pressure changes at take-off and landing.

In the mountains of the Himalayas and the Andes, some people live all their lives at high altitudes. Their bodies become used to the thin air. Their chest and lung capacity is larger than normal and they have more red blood cells to carry extra supplies of oxygen.

▷ Mountaineers breathe supplementary oxygen as they stand on the summit of Everest, the world's tallest peak at 29,035 ft (8,850 m) above sea level. The human body's respiratory system is working at its limit at such heights.

Altitude sickness

This condition is due to lack of oxygen in the body and the low air pressure at high altitudes. It starts with strange feelings of light-headedness, then coughing, headaches, weakness, irregular breathing, loss of appetite and coordination and nausea. There may be palpitations (heart flutters), dizziness, sleeping problems, and swelling of the fingers, toes and face.

Most people are affected by altitude sickness above about 13,000 ft (4,000 m). Its effects can be reduced or even avoided by traveling upward in slow stages, spending some days at each height to allow the body to "acclimatize" (get used to) the new conditions.

Glossary

Allergy: reaction by the body, usually caused by harmless substances to which a person has become oversensitive. Symptoms such as sneezing, watery eyes and rashes may occur.

Alveoli: tiny air sacs in the lungs in which oxygen is absorbed from the air and carbon dioxide is removed from the blood.

Aorta: the largest artery in the body, through which all the blood leaving the left side of the heart passes, to be pumped round the body.

Asthma: disease in which the small airways or bronchioles in the lungs become suddenly narrowed, obstructing the air flow. Asthma may be a form of allergy.

Artery: vessel which carries blood away from the heart.

Bacteria: microscopic organisms, some of which cause disease (like viruses they are often called "germs").

Bronchi: largest airways of the lungs, that branch repeatedly from the bottom of the windpipe (trachea).

Bronchioles: the smallest airways in the lungs, conveying air to the alveoli.

Bronchitis: disease in which the bronchi become inflamed and partly blocked by thick mucus.

Capillaries: the smallest blood vessels. Capillaries penetrate virtually every part of the body and are important in the exchange of oxygen and carbon dioxide in the lungs.

Carbon dioxide: (CO_2) colorless gas produced by the body as a waste product. CO_2 dissolves in the blood and is removed by the lungs.

Carbon monoxide: (CO) colorless gas which is extremely poisonous. CO is found in cigarette smoke and exhaust fumes from automobiles.

Cartilage: whitish, translucent material, which is slightly rubbery. Cartilage cushions joints and is also used to reinforce certain parts of the body.

Cell: the smallest living unit of the body.

Cilia: hair-like structures in the mucous membrane which beat back and forth, producing a current in the mucus.

Diaphragm: tough sheet of muscle separating the organs of the chest from those in the abdomen. The diaphragm plays an important part in breathing.

Emphysema: lung disease in which the alveoli are damaged and no longer function properly, reducing the capacity of the lungs to absorb oxygen.

Epiglottis: small flap in the back of the throat which can block off the entrance to the larynx, preventing food from entering the airways.

Esophagus: the gullet. Tube through which the food is conveyed from the mouth to the stomach.

Expiration: breathing out.

Gas exchange: "swopping" oxygen (which goes from air to blood) and carbon dioxide (from blood to air) in the alveoli of the lungs.

Goblet cells: cup-shaped cells lining the trachea and bronchi (also found elsewhere in the body), which produce sticky mucus.

Hemoglobin: dark red pigment in red blood cells that transports oxygen.

Hay fever: an allergy mostly affecting the eyes and nose. Pollen in the air causes an allergic reaction in which the nose itches and the nose and eyes run very frequently.

Inspiration: breathing in.

Intercostal muscles: sheets of muscle lying between the ribs; used in deep breathing.

Larynx: the voice box or "Adam's apple". The larynx is made from cartilage and is positioned at the front of the throat.

Ligament: tough, ropy

material used to support joints and organs. Ligaments help to hold the diaphram in its relaxed, curved shape.

Lungs: paired, spongy organs in the chest, through which oxygen is absorbed and carbon dioxide is removed from the blood.

Macrophages: large white cells which keep the lungs clean by consuming bacteria and dirt.

Mucous membrane: thin, moist layer covering most of the organs of the body. Mucous membrane lines the trachea, bronchi and bronchioles.

Mucus: sticky liquid secreted by goblet cells in the mucus membrane. Mucus collects and acts as a protective film and lubricant.

Nasal conchae: thin ledges of bone in the nasal cavity which are covered in mucous membrane.

Nicotine: poisonous drug found in cigarette smoke, which can cause a type of addiction.

Oxygen: colorless gas in the air, needed by every cell in the body. In the lungs, oxygen is absorbed into the blood.

Oxyhemoglobin: substance formed when oxygen becomes attached to haemoglobin in the blood. Oxyhaemoglobin is bright red.

Palate: roof of the mouth, divided into the hard and soft palate. The soft palate can seal off the airway to the nasal cavity.

Pharynx: the throat passage through which both food and air travel.

Plasma: clear fluid in which red and white blood cells float.

Pleurae: two thin, slippery membranes which cover the two lungs and fold back on themselves to line the chest cavity.

Pulmonary artery: blood vessel through which blood is pumped from the heart to the lungs.

Pulmonary veins: the four veins, two from each lung, which convey freshly-oxygenated blood back to the left side of the heart.

Respiration: general name for the overall process of absorbing oxygen from the air and using it to "burn" food substances, thereby obtaining energy and releasing carbon dioxide as a waste product. Sometimes used to mean breathing.

Respiratory system: the whole system used in breathing, including the mouth, nose, pharynx, larynx, trachea, bronchi, lungs, diaphragm and intercostal muscles.

Sinuses: air spaces behind the face, in the cheeks and forehead.

Sinusitis: painful blockage of the sinuses, usually caused by an infection such as a cold.

Sternum: the breastbone at the front of the chest, to which most of the ribs are attached.

Trachea: the windpipe, the largest airway. A flexible tube, supported by hoops of cartilage, beginning at the larynx. The two largest bronchi (the principal bronchi) branch from its lower end, one going to each lung.

Turbinates: another form for nasal conchae.

Uvula: soft flap at the back of the soft palate.

Vein: vessel which carries blood back to the heart.

Vena cava: one of the two main veins, bringing blood from the body back to the right side of the heart.

Vocal cords: two tough, shelf-like sheets of shiny mucous membrane stretched across the larynx, which vibrate in the air flow, producing sounds.

Windpipe: common name for the trachea.

Index

PRINTED IN BELGIUM BY

proost
INTERNATIONAL BOOK PRODUCTION